contents

INTRODUCTION

Hello and welcome to Grammar Ray! You are about to enter a world of fun and adventure, where English grammar is brought to life. Words in the English language can be divided into different groups called 'parts of speech'. In this title, we will join the robots in their quest to explore the role of the noun and the pronoun.

I'm Mr Noun, also known as 'The Incredible Noun'. If you enjoy magic and surprises then you are in for a treat.

I am the 'Magnificent Pronoun'. Come and see my powers of transformation and you will hardly believe your eyes!

The first part of the book is a comic strip. Join Mr Noun and Mr Pronoun on stage with some of their friends and witness tricks of grammatical excellence. Look out for the words in blue and orange – they are key to the show.

After you've seen the fantastic show, the rest of the book looks at nouns and pronouns in more detail, and gives some more examples. Use this if you need a reminder of the role nouns and pronouns play in English grammar. It also requires your puzzle-solving skills, and tests what you have learnt along the way. So be sure to pay attention!

a rabbit,

some flowers

and some seeds.

SEEDS

Collective nouns are used to describe groups of things.

For example:

A family,

a band,

a flock of birds,

a deck of cards.

9

height,

surprise,

Aagh!

fear,

inspiration,

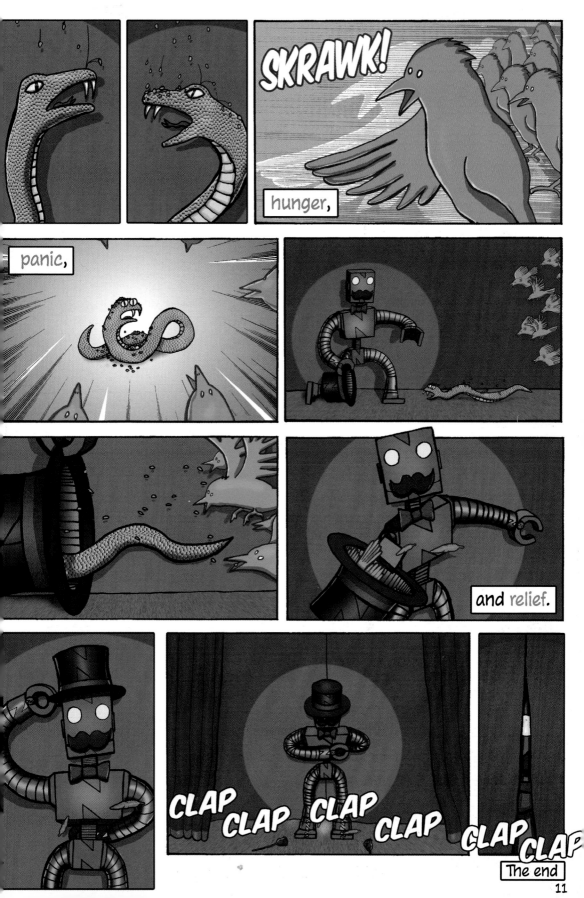

SKRAWK!

hunger,

panic,

and relief.

CLAP CLAP CLAP CLAP CLAP CLAP

The end

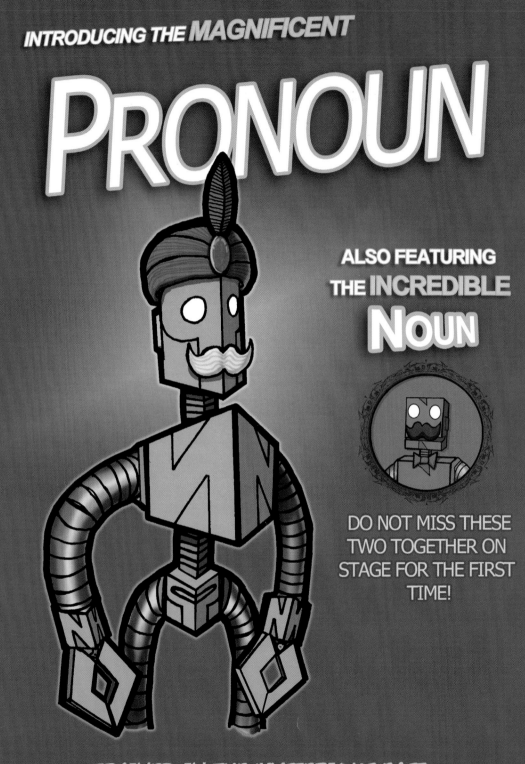

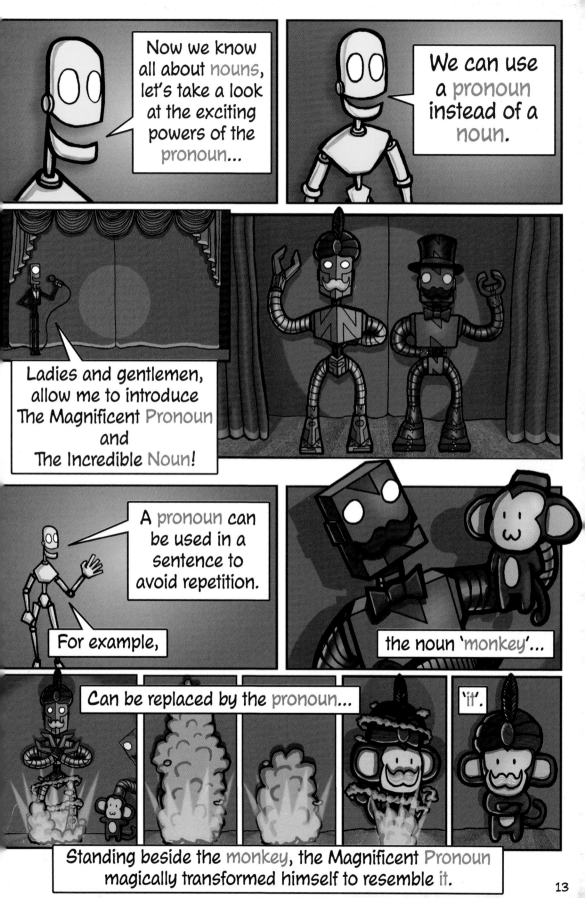

13

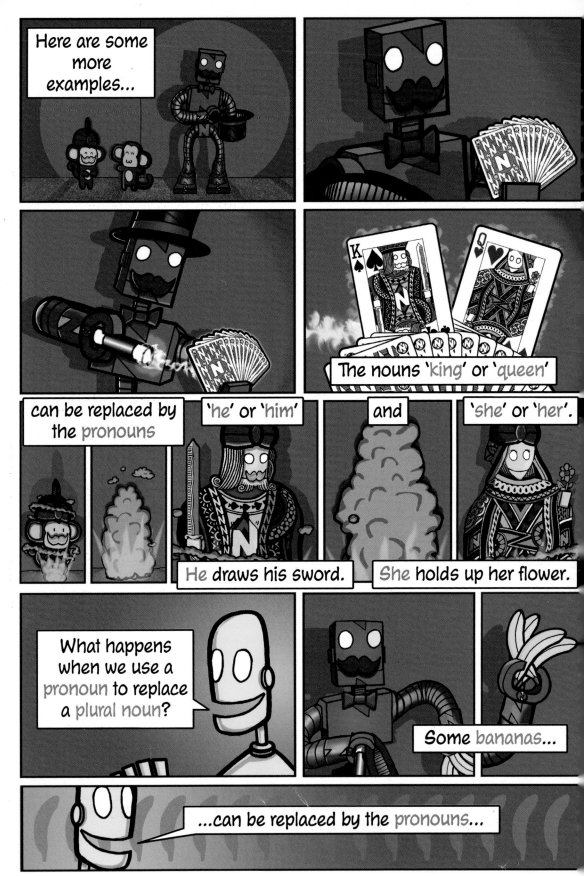

nouns

Nouns are naming words. They can name people, things, places, groups, feelings and ideas. There are four types of basic noun.

COMMON NOUNS

A common noun names everyday things. Unlike a **proper noun** which names specific things (see below), a common noun refers to one of many things which share the same features.

FOR EXAMPLE: *an apple, a computer, a pigeon*

PROPER NOUNS

A proper noun names specific individuals, places, objects or events. All proper nouns begin with a capital letter.

FOR EXAMPLE: *Elvis Presley, Germany, The Statue of Liberty, The Olympic Games*

COLLECTIVE NOUNS

A collective noun names a group of people or things.

FOR EXAMPLE: *an audience, a class, a band, a team, a troop of monkeys, a bunch of grapes*

NOTE: Collective nouns can often be used with more than one type of common noun.

FOR EXAMPLE: *a flock of birds, a flock of sheep, a bunch of grapes, a bunch of flowers*

ABSTRACT NOUNS

An abstract noun names ideas or feelings – things we cannot touch, hear, smell or taste.

FOR EXAMPLE: *joy, truth, excitement, fear, anger, hope*

articles

The words *a, an* and *the* are articles. Articles are small words that often come immediately before nouns. There are two main types of article.

DEFINITE ARTICLE   The word '*the*' is the definite article. We use it when we are talking about specific things.

FOR EXAMPLE: *the Earth, the Pyramids, the Universe*

INDEFINITE ARTICLES   '*A*' and '*an*' are indefinite articles.

We use *an* when the noun starts with a vowel (a, e, i, o, u).

FOR EXAMPLE: *an alligator, an insect, an orange, an idiot*

We use *a* if the noun starts with a consonant (consonants are all the other letters in the alphabet which aren't vowels).

FOR EXAMPLE: *a compass, a turnip, a sandwich, a ball, a magician*

countable and uncountable nouns

Nouns are countable or uncountable.

COUNTABLE NOUNS   A countable noun can be singular (one of) or plural (more than one).

FOR EXAMPLE: a banana   two bananas   three bananas

If we are talking about a noun in the singular form we use the articles *a* or *an.*

FOR EXAMPLE: *a banana, an apricot*

The usual way to show that a noun is plural is to add an -s.

FOR EXAMPLE: *bananas, apricots*

However, there are occasions when this rule does not work. When a noun ends in *-ch, -s, -sh, -ss* or *-x* we add *-es* to make it plural.

Most nouns that finish with *-o* become *-oes* in the plural.

If a noun ends in a consonant followed by *-y*, the plural is different, too. The *-y* changes to *-ies.*

Most, but not all nouns that end in *-f* or *-fe* change to *-ves* in the plural.

FOR EXAMPLE: *church – churches, potato – potatoes, baby – babies, wife – wives*

There are also nouns that are the same in the singular and plural.

FOR EXAMPLE: *one sheep, two sheep; one salmon, two salmon*

When talking about plural nouns we can use a number of words such as *some, many* or *a few* immediately before them.

FOR EXAMPLE: *some bananas, many sheep, a few apricots*

UNCOUNTABLE NOUNS An uncountable noun is singular only and does not have a plural. You do not use a number with an uncountable noun, or the articles *a* and *an*. You can, however, use words such as *some, much,* and *any.*

FOR EXAMPLE: *some water*   *much love*   *any grass*

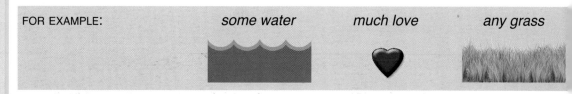

NOUNS
test yourself

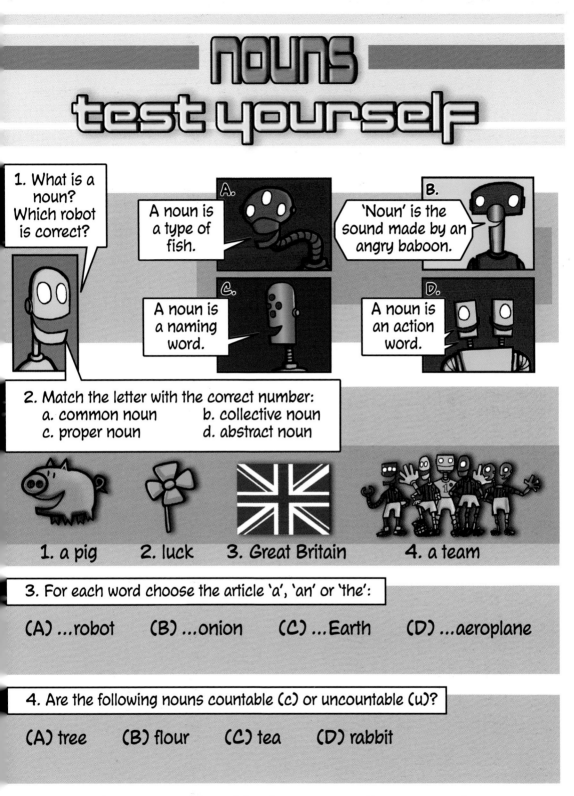

1. What is a noun? Which robot is correct?

A. A noun is a type of fish.

B. 'Noun' is the sound made by an angry baboon.

C. A noun is a naming word.

D. A noun is an action word.

2. Match the letter with the correct number:
a. common noun   b. collective noun
c. proper noun   d. abstract noun

1. a pig   2. luck   3. Great Britain   4. a team

3. For each word choose the article 'a', 'an' or 'the':

(A) ...robot   (B) ...onion   (C) ...Earth   (D) ...aeroplane

4. Are the following nouns countable (c) or uncountable (u)?

(A) tree   (B) flour   (C) tea   (D) rabbit

Turn the page upside-down to see the answers!

(1) C (2) a-1, b-4, c-3, d-2 (3) A-a, B-an, C-the, D-an (4) A-c, B-u, C-u, D-c

more about pronouns

pronouns

**Pronouns are words that we often use to replace nouns.
They are used in sentences to avoid repetition.**

A sentence without the use of a pronoun:

FOR EXAMPLE:

When the <u>monkey</u> climbed the tree, the <u>monkey</u> used the <u>monkey's</u> tail to cling on.

Here is the same sentence, but this time using the pronoun 'it' to replace the noun 'monkey':

FOR EXAMPLE:

When the monkey climbed the tree, <u>it</u> used <u>its</u> tail to cling on.

There are seven types of pronoun, but we will look at the basic four.

PERSONAL PRONOUNS

These are used to refer to people or specific things:
I, me, you, it, he, him, she, her, we, us, they, them, you.

I and *me* are used when referring to yourself.

FOR EXAMPLE:

<u>I</u> was lost but the postman gave <u>me</u> directions.

You is used to refer to someone else you are addressing. It is used in both the singular and plural.

FOR EXAMPLE:

SINGULAR: *Where are <u>you</u> going, Jack?*
PLURAL: *Where are <u>you</u> guys going?*

It is used to replace single nouns – *a crown, a chicken.*

FOR EXAMPLE:

The crown was beautiful and <u>it</u> was covered in diamonds. The chicken was unsure – did <u>it</u> come before the egg?

He or *him* replace male nouns – *a king, a prince.*

FOR EXAMPLE:

When the king went on holiday <u>he</u> forgot to take the queen with <u>him</u>.

She or *her* replace female nouns – *a queen, a princess.*

The princess was angry that <u>she</u> was trapped in the tower without a prince to rescue <u>her</u>.

Use *we* or *us* when referring to yourself or others in a group.

<u>We</u> wanted to go on a picnic but the miserable weather stopped <u>us</u>.

They or *them* replace groups of nouns – *some guards, many monkeys.*

The guards looked scary but <u>they</u> were very friendly when you spoke to <u>them</u>.

POSSESSIVE PRONOUNS

Possessive pronouns are used to indicate ownership and possession: *mine, yours, his, hers, its, ours, theirs.*

That goal was <u>mine</u>, not <u>yours</u>.
Are you sure that dress is <u>hers</u>?
The idea was <u>theirs</u> but he claimed it was <u>his</u>.

DEMONSTRATIVE PRONOUNS

Demonstrative pronouns are used to indicate nouns or pronouns in a sentence: *this, that, these, those.*

This and *these* are used to refer to nouns that are close to us. *That* and *those* refer to nouns that are further away.

<u>That</u> slice of cake is bigger than mine!
Is <u>this</u> the right platform?
I would like <u>this</u> one, not <u>that</u> one.
You take <u>these</u> and I'll carry <u>those</u>.

INTERROGATIVE PRONOUNS

Interrogative pronouns are used to ask questions: *who? what? which? whose?*

<u>Who</u> gave you that cake?   <u>Which</u> is the right platform?
<u>What</u> time is it?   <u>Whose</u> box is that?

pronouns
test yourself

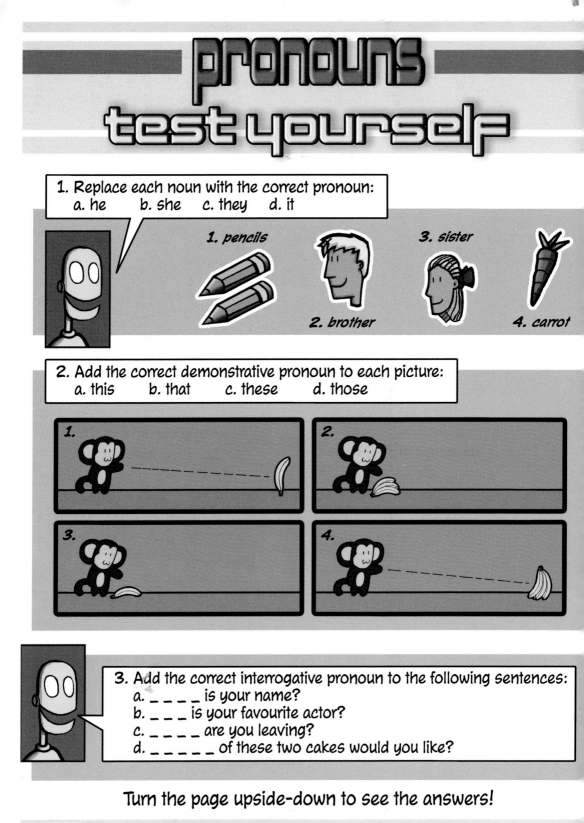

1. Replace each noun with the correct pronoun:
   a. he   b. she   c. they   d. it

1. pencils

2. brother

3. sister

4. carrot

2. Add the correct demonstrative pronoun to each picture:
   a. this   b. that   c. these   d. those

1.

2.

3.

4.

3. Add the correct interrogative pronoun to the following sentences:
   a. _ _ _ _ is your name?
   b. _ _ _ is your favourite actor?
   c. _ _ _ _ are you leaving?
   d. _ _ _ _ _ of these two cakes would you like?

Turn the page upside-down to see the answers!

(1) a-2, b-3, c-1, d-4 (2) a-3, b-1, c-2, d-4
(3) a-What b-Who, c-When, d-Which

INDEX